THE LITTLE BOOK OF

CRAP ADVICE

Mic...

Michael O'Mara Humour

First published in Great Britain in 2001 by
Michael O'Mara Books Limited
9 Lion Yard
Tremadoc Road
London SW4 7NQ

The right of Michael Powell to be identified as the author of this work has
been asserted by him in accordance with the Copyright, Designs and Patents
Act 1988.

A CIP catalogue record for this book is available from the British Library

ISBN 1-85479-883-9

3 5 7 9 10 8 6 4

Designed and typeset by Design 23

Printed and bound in Great Britain by William Clowes, Beccles, Suffolk

How to use this book

There's an exception to every rule, except this one.

Some people say that you should take all the advice you can get. To this end, I've been collecting advice of every kind, from people in all walks of life – advice about work, one's children, escaping from wild animals, staying healthy, protecting one's home, top tv tips, and much more.

I now pass all this advice on to you. My suggestion – simply select the advice that is most relevant to your situation – then ignore it!

As someone once said, 'I may be gullible, but at least I have this magic fish . . .'

The author and the publishers would like to thank all those who submitted material to our regular humour e-mail address:

jokes@michaelomarabooks.com

We always welcome new contributions, but regret that space does not allow for individual credits.

Want that promotion? Need a pay rise? Tried and tested advice for the ambitious employee

Always remember . . .

All power corrupts. Absolute power is pretty cool, though.

If a thing is worth doing, wouldn't it have been done already?

Eagles may soar but weasels don't get sucked into jet engines.

The early bird gets the worm, but the second mouse gets the cheese.

The early bird gets the worm, but the early worm gets eaten.

Ambition is a lame excuse for not having enough sense to be lazy.

Hard work pays off in the future. Laziness pays off now.

Experience is something you don't get until just after you need it.

Doing a job right the first time gets the job done. Doing the job wrong 17 times gives you job security.

Anything worth doing is worth overdoing.

Avoid bickering and petty arguments by immediately punching anyone with whom you disagree.

Get behind early so you have plenty of time to catch up.

Never put off until tomorrow what you can avoid altogether.

When all else fails, lower your standards.

There are three kinds of people: those who can count and those who can't.

To err is human. To really screw things up you need a computer.

A picture may be worth a thousand words, but it uses up a thousand times more memory.

Never let a computer know you're in a hurry.

Give a man a fish and he will eat for a day. Teach him to use the Net and he won't bother you for weeks.

No problem is so big and complicated that it can't be ignored.

Laugh in the face of danger. Then run and hide until it goes away.

There are very few problems that cannot be solved by orders ending with 'or I'll shoot'.

The 50-50-90 rule: when you have a 50-50 chance of getting something right, there's a 90 per cent probability you'll get it wrong.

A pair of lucky dice can often compensate for a lack of good judgement.

If at first you don't succeed, call it a day and have a beer.

Don't use force; use a bigger hammer.

All work and no play makes Jack a dull boy who can retire at 40 and laugh at everyone else slogging away for the next 25 years.

If at first you don't succeed . . .

If you can smile when things go wrong, you already know who you're going to blame.

Before you criticize someone, walk a mile in their shoes. That way you're a mile away, and you have their shoes, too.

If you can stay calm, while all around you is chaos, you probably haven't completely understood the seriousness of the situation.

If you can't beat them, arrange to have them beaten.

If you can't laugh at yourself, make fun of others.

If at first you don't succeed, blame society.

When in doubt, mumble.

Don't be discouraged if you feel a failure. On some days even a hard-on can count as personal growth.

Practice random acts of intelligence and senseless acts of self-control.

Procrastinate now!

Assume full responsibility for your mistakes, except the ones that are someone else's fault.

Never compromise your principles, except to get laid or if there's a chance of a pay rise.

Stop judging others – even the inept and the laughable.

If at first you don't succeed, destroy all evidence that you tried.

And now, some advice from the I.T. department, which you really ought to pay attention to . . .

1. When you call us to have your computer moved, be sure to leave it buried under half a ton of postcards, baby pictures, stuffed animals, dried flowers, darts trophies and children's art. We don't have lives, and we find it deeply moving to catch a fleeting glimpse of yours.

2. Don't write anything down. Ever. We can play back the error messages from here.

3. When I.T. Support sends you an e-mail marked 'High importance', delete it at once. We're just testing.

4. When you call the help desk, state what you want, not what's keeping you from getting it. We don't need to know that you can't get into your mail because your computer won't power up at all.

5. When an I.T. person says he's coming right over, go for coffee. That way you won't be there when we need your password. It's nothing for us to remember 300 screen saver passwords.

6. When an I.T. person is eating lunch at his desk, walk right in and spill your guts right out. We exist only to serve.

7. Send urgent e-mail all in UPPERCASE. The mail server picks it up and flags it as a rush delivery.

8. When the photocopier doesn't work, call computer support. There's electronics in it.

9. When you're getting a 'No dial tone' message at home, call computer support. We can fix your telephone line from here.

10. When you have a dozen old computer screens to get rid of, call computer support. We're collectors.

11. When something's wrong with your home PC, dump it on an I.T. person's chair with no name, no phone number and no description of the problem. We love a puzzle.

12. When an I.T. person tells you that computer screens don't have cartridges in them, argue. We love a good argument.

13. When an I.T. person tells you that he'll be there shortly, reply in a scathing tone of voice, 'And just how many weeks do you mean by shortly?' That motivates us.

14. When the printer won't print, re-send the job at least 20 times. Print jobs frequently get sucked into black holes.

15. When the printer still won't print after 20 tries, send the job to all 68 printers in the company. One of them is bound to work.

16. Don't learn the proper name for anything technical. We know exactly what you mean by 'my thingy blew up'.

17. Don't use on-line help. On-line help is for wimps.

18. If the mouse cable keeps knocking down the framed picture of your dog, lift the computer and stuff the cable under it. Mouse cables were designed to have 25 lbs of computer sitting on top of them.

19. If the space bar on your keyboard doesn't work, blame it on the e-mail upgrade. Keyboards are actually very happy with half a pound of cake crumbs and nail clippings in them.

20. When you get a message saying 'Are you sure?' click on that 'Yes' button as fast as you can. Hell, if you weren't sure, you wouldn't be doing it, would you?

21. When you find an I.T. person on the phone with his bank, sit uninvited on the corner of his desk and stare at him until he hangs up. We don't have any money to speak of anyway.

22. Feel perfectly free to say things like, 'I don't know nothing about that computer crap'. We don't mind at all hearing our area of professional expertise referred to as crap.

23. When you need to change the toner cartridge in a printer, call I.T. Support. Changing a toner cartridge is an extremely complex task and manufacturers recommend that it be performed only by a professional engineer with a masters degree in nuclear physics.

24. When your computer won't power up, complain to us before you check to see whether you've switched on the monitor.

25. When you have a lock to pick on an old filing cabinet, call I.T. Support. We love to hack.

26. When something's the matter with your computer, ask your secretary to call the help desk. We enjoy the challenge of having to deal with a third party who doesn't know anything about the problem.

27. When you receive a 30MB (huge) movie file, send it to everyone as an e-mail attachment. We've got lots of disk space on that mail server.

28. Don't even think of breaking large print jobs down into smaller chunks. Somebody else might get a chance to squeeze a memo into the queue.

29. When an I.T. person gets in the lift pushing £60,000 worth of computer equipment on a trolley, ask in a very loud voice: 'Good grief, you take the elevator to go DOWN one floor?!' That's another one that cracks us up no end.

30. When you lose your car keys, send an e-mail to the entire company. People out in the Isle of Man office like to keep abreast of what's going on.

31. When you bump into an I.T. person in the supermarket on a Saturday, ask a computer question. We do weekends.

32. Don't bother to tell us when you move computers around on your own. Computer names are just a cosmetic feature.

33. When you bring your own personal home PC for repair at the office, leave the documentation at home. We'll find all the settings and drivers somewhere.

Say a little prayer . . .

Grant me the grace to accept the things I cannot change,
The courage to change the things I cannot accept,
And the wisdom to forgive those I had to viciously assault today because they got right in my face.

Help me to always give 100 per cent at work:
15 per cent on Monday, 25 per cent on Tuesday, 35 per cent on Wednesday, 20 per cent on Thursday, and 5 per cent on Friday.

And help me always to disguise those things
that I left undone that I should have done by 5 p.m.
And let me not forget, when the world is against me
And everybody seems to be getting on my tits,
That it takes forty-two muscles to frown
And only four to raise my middle finger
and tell them where they can shove their stinking job.

Why does it always seem to be you? Perhaps it's not – and if it's not you, then it must be everyone else . . .

Hell *is* other people

In order to unravel the paradox that is mankind, we should examine the word itself: 'Mankind'. Interestingly, it consists of two separate words – 'mank' and 'ind'. What do these words mean? It's an enigma and so is mankind. 'Politics' also consists of two words, 'poly' meaning 'many' and 'ticks' as in 'tiny bloodsucking parasites'.

Never hit a man with glasses, use a baseball bat.

Learn to love the personality flaws of others – for some it's the only personality they have.

Help a man when he is in trouble and he will remember you the next time he is in trouble.

If you can keep your head when all around you are losing theirs, try landing your helicopter somewhere quieter.

Don't kick a man when he's down unless you're certain he won't get up.

A friend is someone who has the same enemies you have.

Make it idiot proof and someone will make a better idiot.

Dead men don't bite. But pretty soon they start to smell.

Half the people in the world are below average.

Be nice to the nerds and loners at school. You'll be working for them in the future.

When you go to court, your future is decided by twelve people who weren't clever enough to get out of jury service.

Love your neighbours and love your enemies – they're probably one and the same.

When you feel like killing someone, instead of doing something you'll regret later, here's a neat little trick to calm you down. Go over to the person's house and leave a pumpkin lantern on their doorstep with a big kitchen knife sticking in its head and a note saying 'You're next'. It will make you feel much better and no harm done.

. . . or is it other people's children? Advice for parents

A father is someone who carries pictures where his money used to be.

When your child wants to know where rain comes from, tell him that God is crying because of something he did.

Never raise your hands to your children. It leaves your groin unprotected.

No matter how you try to protect your kids, they will eventually get arrested and end up in the local paper.

Children need encouragement. If your child gets an answer right, tell him it was a lucky guess. That way he develops a good, lucky feeling.

To help your small children find you in a public place, periodically fire a starting pistol into the air.

When he's older, tell him he used to have a brother, but he didn't obey.

The face of a child can say it all, especially the mouth part of the face.

If he has a nightmare about monsters, give him a gun and encourage him to fire off a few rounds under his bed whenever he gets scared.

Making your child eat gravel will encourage a regular toothcare regime. Explain that birds have to do this because they haven't got any teeth, so you'd better look after yours etc.

Children need to feel secure. So strap them down whenever possible.

Allow children to learn by making their own mistakes. Laughing at their stupidity also helps.

Children need plenty of space. So leave them home alone at every opportunity.

Encourage independence by regularly losing them in the supermarket.

Children need to feel wanted. Each night, stagger pissed into their bedroom at 2 a.m. and wake them up to tell them you love them. Hug them tightly and start crying uncontrollably.

Teach children the value of money by making sure they always know how much they are costing you.

Avoid embarrassing them in front of their peers by forbidding them ever to bring friends home.

Avoid pester power by using a little reverse psychology. Buy everything that they demand. The novelty of having every material need pandered to will soon wear off and when your kids grow up they'll give away all their possessions and go and work for UNICEF.

Foster problem-solving skills in young children by inventing imaginative scenarios to encourage them to think laterally. For example, pretend to have a heart attack on the kitchen floor and see whether they have the presence of mind to call for an ambulance. Be prepared to lie on the floor for several days, because sometimes children react in the funniest of ways.

Save up any food they don't eat and present it to them on their 21st birthday. As the truck arrives, explain that many people in this world are starving. Then tell them they can't leave home until they've eaten every last scrap.

Advice you wish they had – or hadn't – taken!

There'll be much more leg room in the back, President Kennedy.
ONE OF JFK'S AIDES

If you're ever in Alexandria, you should look up Cleopatra.
JULIUS CAESAR TO MARK ANTONY

You could do a lot worse than eat at Lucretia's.
CESARE BORGIA TO MICHELANGELO

Nobody's interested in your mother!
JOHN RUSKIN TO AMERICAN ARTIST J.A.M. WHISTLER

With the Italian army behind you, the war will be over by spring.
BENITO MUSSOLINI TO ADOLF HITLER

You'll never get anywhere in life sitting under that apple tree all day!
MRS NEWTON TO HER SON, ISAAC

Don't forget to check on the oven!
HOUSEWIFE OF THE YEAR, EATHELBURGHA TO ALFRED THE GREAT

Moscow's lovely in winter.
MARSHAL NEY TO THE EMPEROR NAPOLEON

Stop hogging the bathroom and take a shower!
EUCLID TO FLATMATE ARCHIMEDES

Well, Mr Jack: fine gentleman like you, smart
surgeon's bag – yer'll be more comfortable round at
my place . . .
LONG LIZ STRIDE TO UNKNOWN GENTLEMAN

If you go down to the woods today, you probably
won't see a soul.
THEODORE ROOSEVELT

Want to live long and prosper? Do you need the body of someone half your age? Proven advice for the health conscious

A healthy body . . .

Eat healthily, exercise daily, think positively, die anyway.

Gargle every day to see if your throat leaks.

Don't work out. No pain, no pain.

Learn from your parents' mistakes – use birth control.

Never play leap frog with a unicorn.

If your eyes hurt after you drink coffee, remove the spoon from the cup.

Don't sit on the sofa all day watching TV. Watch it in bed for a change.

If life gives you lemons, stick them down your shirt and make your boobs look bigger.

When jogging at night, be safe: shine a torch into the eyes of passing motorists to ensure you can be seen.

Give a man a fish and he will eat for a day. Teach him how to fish, and he will sit in a boat and drink beer all week.

Don't drink and drive. Do all your drinking before you get into the car.

Increase your life expectancy by living longer.

Live dangerously. Skate on the underside of the ice.

Save matches: chain smoke.

Weigh an empty coke can. Then open a new can and weigh it in between sips. Stop drinking when your can weighs the same as the empty can.

Obtain a wrinkle-free appearance by rapidly gaining a hundred pounds. That's if you don't mind the stretch marks.

A balanced diet is a cake in each hand.

To avoid the chore of slicing bread, buy bread that is already sliced.

Liven up dried spaghetti by boiling it in a pan of water before eating.

Red meat isn't bad for you. Furry grey meat is bad for you.

Always wait at least an hour after eating before you stick your tongue in an electrical socket.

One man's meat is another man's meat, after seventy-two hours of pioneering surgery.

Many drops make a shower, but many showers indicate that someone has a personal hygiene problem.

He who visits the men's room with no shoes, returns with wet feet.

Three things to do when you wake up with a hangover

1. Look in the mirror. Your face will be familiar, even if you can't remember the name.

2. Tell yourself you are simply experiencing the wrath of grapes.

3. Always listen to what your Rice Krispies are trying to tell you.

. . . and a healthy mind . . .

Don't waste time reliving the past when you can spend it worrying about the future.

Smile in the face of adversity – and adversity will probably think you're taking the piss and beat the crap out of you.

Remember that it takes a big man to cry, but it takes a bigger man to laugh at that man.

Remember that no matter where you go, there you are.

It may be that your sole purpose in life is simply to serve as a warning to others.

Smile. It's the second-best thing you can do with your lips.

Honesty is the best policy, but insanity is a better defence.

Abandon the search for Truth – settle for a good fantasy.

Always yield to temptation, because it may not pass your way again.

Never go to bed mad, stay up and fight.

Don't let people drive you crazy when you know it's within walking distance.

Feel the fear and – stay under the sheets.

Nostalgia ain't what it used to be.

Always be sincere, even if you don't mean it.

It is easier to get forgiveness than permission.

Do unto others before they do unto you.

Laugh at your problems – imagine them happening to someone else.

If something was meant to be, it usually never happens.

The things that come to those who wait are the things those who got there first didn't want.

Don't do it if you can't keep it up.

Just because you're paranoid doesn't mean that they aren't after you.

Boycott shampoo! Demand the REAL poo!

Do not suffer in silence, if you can make others suffer with you.

Remember all of you is beautiful and valuable – even the ugly, stupid, and worthless bits.

Make a list of your faults today – then it will be easier to blame them all on your parents tomorrow.

Don't forget that depression is merely anger without enthusiasm.

Live every day as if it is your last. Eventually you'll be right.

BITE THIS!

How to deal with love and sex in the Noughties . . .

You cannot make someone love you. All you can do is stalk them and hope they panic and give in.

There is no remedy for sex but more sex.

Love your neighbour, but don't get caught.

The best way to a man's heart is to saw his chest open.

How to satisfy a woman

Adore, appreciate, beguile, captivate, caress, charm, cherish, coax, commit to, compliment, console, delight, embrace, empathize, enchant, enthral, hug, humour, idolize, indulge, massage, nuzzle, palpitate, pamper, phone, placate, promise, relish, respect, sacrifice for, savour, serenade, spoil, stroke, treasure, understand, venerate, worship.

How to satisfy a man

Show up naked.

Useless with numbers? Always short of cash? Some handy maths advice

Find a penny and pick it up, and all day long you'll have a penny.

The quickest way to double your money is to fold it in half and put it back in your pocket.

A fool and his money are soon partying.

It is morally wrong to allow suckers to keep their money.

If money can't buy you love, rent it.

Save the lids from jam jars and milk bottle tops and use them as currency.

Metric Proverbs

Give a man 2.5 centimetres and he'll take 1.6 kilometres.

Put your best 0.3 of a metre forward.

A miss is as good as 1.6 kilometres.

28 grammes of prevention is worth 453 grammes of cure.

Spare the 5.03 metres and spoil the child.

An Englishman's home is his castle – how to live like a king and sod the rest of yer!

Those who live in glass houses should change in the basement.

You can't have everything. Where would you put it?

A used washing-up liquid container with the top cut off makes a stylish cocktail umbrella stand.

Keep used oil from the chip pan for greasing long distance swimmers.

Save money on heating by covering your walls with tin foil.

Keep flies out of your lounge. Leave a bucket of horse manure in your kitchen.

Impress your neighbours by leaving broken white goods such as fridges and washing machines in your front garden. They will think you have just splashed out on a smart new kitchen.

Silence a dripping tap by sticking your fingers in your ears.

To stop ashtrays from smelling, encourage guests to flick ash on your carpet.

Pour 25 kgs of salt into your pond to prevent your prized collection of freshwater carp from freezing to death.

To prevent your toilet from smelling, urinate in the bath.

Place an old hub cap at the end of a sticky tape roll to make it easier to find.

To stop chairs from making dent marks on the floor, hang them from the ceiling using strong metal wire.

Cut a big hole in the top of your umbrella to stop it blowing away in the wind.

To prevent a small bag from slipping down your arm, paint a tennis ball the same colour as your outfit and attach it to the top of your shoulder.

Stop car locks from freezing by filling them with superglue.

Reduce condensation in your bathroom by only bathing in cold water.

A handsome book collection is often personal and difficult to replace. Copy each book and keep it somewhere safe.

To avoid hitting the wall at the back of your garage when driving your car in, place broken glass six feet in front. When you hear the sound of air escaping rapidly from your front tyres, you know it's time to stop.

Remove the top five rungs from your ladder to make it safer.

Before packing away your Christmas tree decorations, smash one of the lights. Then next year you won't have to waste time figuring out which one isn't working.

Housewives: buy a Global Positioning System, an expensive hi-tech electronic device used by the army and even the SAS. Then when you are shopping, you'll know your exact position on the planet to within one metre of accuracy.

Take the guesswork out of remembering who you have lent stuff to by rubbing your belongings with a highly radioactive material (available at most municipal rubbish tips). Then use a Geiger counter to track down your belongings.

Avoid a dirty tide mark around the inside of your bath by always filling it until it overflows.

Don't throw away old toothbrushes. They are ideal for cleaning the corridors and decks of large military ships.

Let people know where you stand – wear the same socks for a month.

If the shoe fits, get another one just like it.

Avoid lengthy supermarket queues by always choosing the till with the fewest people.

Always keep a full petrol can in your garage in case you run out on a long journey.

When others want what you have: nine ways to keep it safe

Buy a police car and park it in your drive.

Make your house look uninhabited. Board up the windows. Leave a burned out fridge on the lawn. Paint graffiti on the walls. Dig a tunnel to enable you to gain access to your house without having to use the front door. Then sit back and enjoy the lifestyle that you have worked so hard for.

Put a sign saying, 'I am a criminal' in your front window. A criminal will never steal from another criminal (except his mother).

Chain a vicious dog or poisonous snake to everything of value.

Nail a magpie to your front door. Burglars are notoriously superstitious.

Urinate (women) or ejaculate (men) on all your possessions. The police can then use DNA tracing to identify stolen property.

Hire a crane and suspend a huge glass dome above your house. Burglars will avoid a property with a conspicuous security device.

Pepper antipersonnel mines around your garden. However, this can be inconvenient if you have children or pets.

As it is on TV or in the movies so it is in life. Learning from experience; or, Never judge a book by its movie

If you crash your car it will always explode.

If you are a teenager, you will die horribly after having sex.

You must pick up your phone after the first ring or the other person will assume you are out and hang up.

If you are a woman who is running away from someone you will trip and fall.

Drivers: avoid being attacked by a *Tyrannosaurus rex* by keeping a glass of water on your dashboard. The sudden appearance of rhythmical ripples on the surface of the water will provide ample warning that a large dinosaur is approaching.

If you succeed in killing a monster, never check to see if it's really dead.

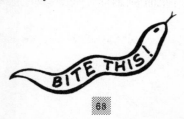

BITE THIS!

Never search the basement, especially during a power cut.

If you are in a high-speed car chase, you will always encounter the following obstacles: a blind man, a street vendor selling fruit, a one-way street, a pile of empty cardboard boxes, a wobbly old man on a bike carrying a string of onions and finally, a sign saying 'Bridge ahead incomplete'.

Move to New York as everyone can afford huge studio apartments, regardless of their income.

If you start dancing in the street, everyone else will know all the steps.

A car won't start trying to knock you off the road until immediately after you spot it in your rear-view mirror.

When they are alone, all foreigners prefer to speak English to one another.

At least one of a pair of identical twins is born evil.

Cars always skid around corners.

Should you decide to defuse a bomb, don't worry which wire to cut. You will always choose the right one.

Most laptop computers are powerful enough to override the communications system of any invading alien society.

It does not matter if you are heavily outnumbered in a fight involving martial arts – your enemies will wait patiently to attack you one by one by dancing around in a threatening manner until you have knocked out their predecessors.

Bad guys always shoot worse than good guys.

When you turn out the light to go to bed, everything in your bedroom will still be clearly visible, just slightly bluish.

If you are blonde and pretty, it is possible to become a world expert on nuclear fission at the age of 22.

Honest and hard-working policemen are traditionally gunned down three days before their retirement.

During all police investigations, it will be necessary to visit a strip club at least once.

All grocery shopping bags contain at least one stick of French bread.

All beds have special L-shaped cover sheets that reach up to the armpit level on a woman but only to waist level on the man lying beside her.

Anyone can land a plane providing there's someone in the control tower to talk you down.

Once applied, lipstick will never rub off – even while scuba diving.

You're very likely to survive any battle in any war unless you make the mistake of showing someone a picture of your sweetheart back home.

Should you wish to pass yourself off as a German or Russian officer, it will not be necessary to speak the language. A German or Russian accent will do.

The Eiffel Tower can be seen from any window in Paris.

A man will show no pain while taking the most ferocious beating but will wince when a woman tries to clean his wounds.

If staying in a haunted house, women should investigate any strange noises in their most revealing underwear.

Word processors never display a cursor on screen but will always say: Enter Password Now.

Even when driving down a perfectly straight road, it is necessary to turn the steering wheel vigorously from left to right every few moments.

All bombs are fitted with electronic timing devices with large red readouts so you know exactly when they're going to go off. (In the *Conglomerated Bombmakers Of The World Handbook*, page 7, paragraph 3: All bombs, made for public display and/or filming, shall have a LED/LCD readout for filming, theatrical suspense, and to make the actors look good.)

A detective can only solve a case once he has been suspended from duty.

Police departments give their officers personality tests to make sure they are deliberately assigned a partner who is their total opposite.

If you are being chased in a city, you can usually blend into a crowd of carnival revellers.

And finally: if you chant 'Jerry! Jerry! Jerry!' loud enough, the lesbian stripper always takes her top off.

The Four Laws of Cartoons

1. Anyone suspended in space will remain in space until made aware of their position.

2. Anyone passing through solid matter will leave a breach concomitant with their periphery.

3. A cat will take on the shape of its container.

4. Everything falls faster than an anvil.

Never owned a pet? Couldn't afford Barbara Woodhouse? Here's how to deal with animals

Never look a gift horse in the mouth. But do encourage it to crap on your roses.

A barking dog never bites. But it can still dump on your doorstep.

If you can't teach an old dog new tricks, you probably need to turn up the voltage.

If a pit bull humps your leg, you'd better fake an orgasm.

The hare is quicker than the tortoise, but the tortoise is uglier.

Save the whales. Collect the whole set.

Don't count your chickens until they've crossed the road.

Birds of a feather flock together and crap on your car.

If after a disaster you have to leave town, take your pets with you. They are unlikely to survive on their own and can break the monotony when the tinned food runs out.

If you're a horse, and someone gets on you, and falls off, and then gets right back on you, buck him off straight away.

A foolproof method for sculpting an elephant
First, get a huge block of marble. Then, chip away everything that doesn't look like an elephant.

How to escape attacks from wild animals (probably)

Attack from an unfriendly lion

Wait until the lion is five feet away and then ram a large pair of step ladders down its throat. If you cannot locate any step ladders in the jungle, then a small item of furniture such as a bedside table or a cocktail cabinet will do.

Charge by an enraged bull

Bulls have notoriously weak bladders, so make the sound of running water, or begin to urinate yourself, and the bull will stop dead to take a leak.

Crocodile attack

Look it straight in the eye, then stick out your tongue to touch the tip of your nose. A crocodile cannot stick out its tongue but it will be so impressed that it will try to copy you, causing its tongue to snap off. Then it will bleed to death.

Seized by a gorilla

Go very limp and start to make little purring noises. The gorilla will think you are a female gorilla. He will roll you over and have rough sex with you after which he will fall asleep, allowing you to make his breakfast and then escape unscathed.

Attack by a buzzard

Get a hobby! Buzzards are only attracted to dead meat.

Swallowed by a killer whale

Motorways are routinely patrolled by traffic police who will quickly come to your aid. Do not attempt to escape from the whale's stomach yourself as you could become disorientated and stagger into oncoming traffic. Use your mobile phone if you are a woman on your own.

Elephant stampede

Blend seamlessly into the herd by putting your nose on your shoulder and waving your arm in front of you. The stampeding elephants will then run around you.

Attack by a shark

Jam an oxygen cylinder into the shark's mouth, then fire at it with your last bullet.

Attack by shoal of piranhas

Get out of the water, asshole.

Bear attack

Pretend to be a fish. The bear will bang your head against a rock to stun you. Then at least you won't feel anything when it rips both your arms off.

Listen to what the voices are telling you
Advice for daily living

Gun control: use both hands.

When using a toilet on a busy train, avoid the embarrassment and irritation of strangers trying the door by leaving it open. That way everyone can see that you are taking a dump and that they should wait their turn.

Fool people into thinking you are enlightened by smiling enigmatically whenever anyone punches you in the face.

Avoid the inconvenience of getting dog muck on the bottom of your shoes by crawling everywhere on your hands and knees.

If you're sitting next to Elvis Presley on a bus and suddenly a large flat fish with orange spots and a leather jacket sits down on the other side, then you're between a rocker and a hard plaice.

Remember that a clear conscience is usually the sign of a weak memory.

If you must choose between two evils, pick the one you've never tried before.

Plan to be spontaneous tomorrow.

Light travels faster than sound. That's why some people appear bright until you hear them speak.

Conscience is what hurts when everything else feels so good.

If it ain't broke, fix it till it is.

It's frustrating when you know all the answers, but nobody bothers asking you the questions.

Avoid the embarrassment of tripping in public by repeating the same movement several times to make it look like a normal part of your behaviour.

The only substitute for good manners is fast reflexes.

Always remember you're unique, just like everyone else.

Avoid unsightly wear marks on the elbows of your favourite jacket by cutting them out and leaving them in your wardrobe.

Remember the nice thing about egotists is that they don't talk about other people.

Never underestimate the power of stupid people in large groups.

Fool your friends into thinking you are a member of the aristocracy by buying a large stately home in the country surrounded by four hundred acres of land.

Men are from earth. Women are from earth. Deal with it.

Go ahead and take risks. Just be sure that everything will turn out OK.

If you can't be kind, at least have the decency to be vague.

The easiest way to find something lost around the house is to buy a replacement.

If you think there is good in everybody, you haven't met everybody.

Living on earth is expensive, but it does include a free trip around the sun.

Find humour in every day – find someone to laugh at.

Don't bother voting. If it could change things, do you really think it would be legal?

It's hard to make a comeback when you haven't been anywhere.

Remember the only difference between a rut and a grave is the depth.

Those who live by the sword get shot by those who don't.

Just remember, if the world didn't suck, we'd all fall off.

It's bad luck to walk under a bladder.

You can get more with a kind word and a gun, than just a kind word.

Opportunity knocks but once – and then shoots through the letterbox.

If you want to find Jesus, try to remember where you last saw him. But he's usually stuck down the side of the sofa.

The meek will inherit the earth, after everyone else has finished with it.

Many people have fallen by the edge of the sword, but many more have gone over on their ankle.

If you're in a war, instead of throwing a hand grenade at the enemy, throw flowers. Maybe it will make them stop to consider how nonsensical and destructive war is. And while they are thinking, you can throw a real grenade at them.

You will catch more flies with a bucket of crap than with a spoonful of honey.

Democracy is too good to share with everybody.

Jesus loves you, but everyone else thinks you're a twat.

Never knock on Death's door – ring the doorbell and run.

He who laughs last just got the joke.

All Michael O'Mara titles are available by post from:

Bookpost, P.O. Box 29, Douglas, Isle of Man IM99 1BQ

Credit cards accepted. Please telephone 01624 836000
Fax 01624 837033
Internet http://www.bookpost.co.uk
e-mail bookshop@enterprise.net

Free postage and packing in the UK.
Overseas customers allow £1 per book (paperbacks)
and £3 per book (hardbacks)

Other Little Books:
The Little Book of Farting - ISBN 1-85479-445-0
The Little Book of Stupid Men - ISBN 1-85479-454-X
The Little Toilet Book - ISBN 1-85479- 456-6
The Little Book of Venom - ISBN 1-85479-446-9
The Little Book of Pants - ISBN 1-85479-477-9
The Little Book of Pants 2 - ISBN 1-85479-557-0
The Little Book of Bums - ISBN 1-85479-561-9
The Little Book of Revenge - ISBN 1-85479-562-7
The Little Book of Voodoo - ISBN 1-85479-560-0
The Little Book of Blondes - ISBN 1-85479-558-9
The Little Book of Magical Love Spells -
    ISBN 1-85479-559-7

The Little Book of Cockney Rhyming Slang -
   ISBN 1-85479-825-1
The Little Book of Gay Gags - ISBN 1-85479-590-2
The Little Book of Irish Grannies' Remedies -
   ISBN 1-85479-828-6
The Little Book of Scottish Grannies' Remedies -
   ISBN 1-85479-829-4
The Little Book of Irish Wit and Wisdom -
   ISBN 1-85479-827-8
The Little Book of Scottish Wit and Wisdom -
   ISBN 1-85479-826-X
The Little Book of Popney Rhyming Slang -
   ISBN 1-85479-819-7
The Little Book of the SAS - ISBN 1-85479-887-1
101 Really Unpleasant Things About Men -
   ISBN 1-85479-881-2
Get Your Coat - You've Pulled - ISBN 1-85479-891-X
The Little Book of Crap Excuses - ISBN 1-85479-882-0
The Little Book of Totally Stupid Men -
   ISBN 1-85479-833-2
The Little Couch Potato Book - ISBN 1-85479-834-0
Welcome to Dumpsville - ISBN 1-85479-880-4
The Little Book of Despair - ISBN 1-85479-818-9
The Little Book of Sex Fantasies - ISBN 1-85479-725-5
The Little Book of Tantric Sex For Busy People -
   ISBN 1-85479-685-2